JUST OUTSIDE

Barbara Schmitz

For information about permission to reproduce selections from this book, contact *Permissions*, Sandhills Press loupvalley@yahoo.com

Printed in the United States of America
Sandhills Press
Ord, NE ⁓ Nacogdoches, TX

Cover art: "Tree of Life," by Markella Hatizano.
Author photo: Karen Wingett

Acknowledgments

"Why I Became a Vegetarian," *Pinyon Review.*

"October 1945" and "When I Think of a Landscape," *Memory, Echo, Words: Scurfpea Anthology, 2014.*

"Listening to the Trees," *The Scandalous Life of Butterflies: Scurfpea Anthology, 2015.*

"Packing Her Up" and "Porch Talks," in *Watching the Perseids: The Backwaters Press Twentieth Anniversary Anthology* (2017)

"Practice," "Rescue," and "When you Speak" were also included in *What Bob Says (Some More)* from WSC Press, 2018.

Thank you to Greg Kosmicki for reading "Just Outside" while the manuscript was being finished. Special thanks to Mark Sanders for "seeing" my poetry from the beginning, Northern Lights Writing Group where most of these poems "came out," The Cabin Girls for support, love, and all the creative energy at quarterly retreats, Sweetheart Bob, the ultimate in poet's companions.

CONTENTS

III. JUST OUTSIDE

For Makena, Her Majesty the Queen of Happiness...

TAKING OUT THE TRASH

EARLY MORNING,
TAKING OUT THE TRASH

I greet the setting moon
at the end of the drive—
enormous round face
of pale light.
I blow kisses.
She smiles secretly.

Lying about in exhausted collapse,
golden leaves remind of last night's
orgy—thunder, lightning, climaxing
rain. Air snaps enough to make
you tip your hat, but not yet
reach for a jacket.

How I love this tart,
Autumn, with her exuberant
exhibitionism, showing off her
brilliant quick-change costumes
before she drops
them all in a fit for us
to tidy up.

THE MASSAGE

"All the angels are here," says the masseuse
after tugging a long blue string out of
my shoulder. "Old attachments," she explains.
I do not see where she discarded my old
hurts but they are *Gate' Gate' Parasangate'*
Gone Gone like the river   the winter   memories
of love making   mother   father   friends who
departed before spring. "Feel better?" she asks.
A hollow bell, I ring.

DAYLIGHT SAVINGS

I

6:30!
Ah! Slept all night
    I congratulate myself
    Check the electronic
        bank sign out the window
Oh, no! It's 5:30
    that saving daylight/saving
    time maneuver we do
    in fall and spring trying to
    move light from in front to behind

Well, who invented time?
    my mother asked during
    one of these transitions
*Didn't God? Why don't we
    leave it alone?*
I think it was the Phoenicians,
    I say

I always loved tranquil
        gardens with sundials
        and the sun's gentle arrow
        marking off a sliver of life
        on a sculpted wheel set
        amongst the flowers

Driving home from the city
        last night in the final
        summer early night light—
tonight it'll be pitch dark at
        this hour—my husband

asks, *Did you see something,*
beside the road (once we
crashed into a steer escaped
its pen)   *No,* I say, *just a shadow*—
just daytime/nighttime having
a last kiss goodbye

II

I was all prepared to
        lose an hour
It's that time of life
        hair thinning
        face no longer so
            bright in photos
I work daily at turning
            resignation into acceptance

But, it's Fall!
        and being up a short time
        I discover I've really
        gained an hour
    (have trouble keeping numbers,
        anything scientific. straight
        in my heavily-tipped right brain)

So now it's like
        birthday money
        unexpected
        to spend how-I-wish
        even on something foolish

I eat lots of bread

GREW UP

When I grew up
we had to wear
dresses to school
Leggings were slacks
we wore underneath
took off with our boots
We had to cover
our heads at Mass
(sometimes a bobby-pinned doily)
Always had an Easter hat,
short pastel spring coat,
patent leather shoes
we thought we deserved
after giving up candy
all of Lent and all
those Stations of the Cross
on our knees   Gloomy
purple coverings pulled off
statues of Mary, St. Jude
for Easter-lily morning
Bells clanging and Jesus
or the Bunny rising up
early to fill our woven
baskets with chocolate
marshmallow eggs

NOT SO GOOD

Hang on, I say at Hy-Vee when
the clerk in the Express Lane
asks for my Fuel Saver number
when I'm trying to enter debit
card digits in the machine *I can't*
think of two numbers at once She
waits kindly not acting exasperated
Sometimes I can't get the right number
even if no one is asking me another
and have it written down on a tiny
slip of paper in my foldout wallet
my husband wants me to replace but
It works all right; why get new when
the old one is working I always said
that too about my second-hand range
with the oven door which wouldn't
stay latched and kept hitting him on
the head when he tried to light the
pilot light which kept going out Finally
he picked out a new stove but we had
to take it back because the roasting pan
which had belonged to his mother that
I always cooked Thanksgiving turkey in
wouldn't fit Now I've lost the manual
for my second new range my husband
says we paid too much for but I was afraid
of getting "A piece of crap" I love that
Neil Young song about all the plastic shit
advertised on TV you can send for and it's
no good but husband was loyal to shyster
appliance salesman who sold us our Irish
setter forty years ago and everything we've
bought from him has something wrong with it
The new dryer wouldn't work and he kept

sending repairmen until I went to his store
every day at lunch time when he was trying
to eat his sandwich and insisted he take
the lemon back   Kept the refrigerator
with its nicks and cuts on the side after
he talked us into it telling us they were
phasing out the models with the freezer
at the bottom and this side by side was what
people wanted now   Old one broken down
we were keeping our stuff in a cooler so
we said *Oh, all right* sort of believing him
but the clerk smiles says it's okay when
I explain my generation is not so good
at multitasking My son insists he is
great at it but I read an article stating
people are not as good as they think they
are I don't think it was on the internet
either   Maybe it was

STAR UNRAVELS

It didn't
know
it was a star
Cold and lonely
Heavy   Nowhere
to lie down

At the bottom
of a gully
a small song
throbs from what's
left of its splintered
        heart

BE TREE   (title of a poem by Natalie Goldberg)

"You don't write about the land," he criticized.

I write about my walnut tree's faithfulness
her alive pulsing heart disguised under bark
pumping valentines
vibrating tender notes
  to us inside she protects
  in vulnerable sleep and sexual positions
No questions
Rare love
  Nothing asked

DOWSING

My father could dowse for water
"How did he learn to do that?"
                    one friend asks
I never thought to ask   So many
things we didn't ask
                    each other

This father who was husking corn
                    by hand in the field
                    with mules
when Lindberg flew across
                    the Atlantic
His sister would come out
                    with water
                    with sandwiches
to give him a radio report

His daughter—about the same age—
watched the Moon Landing
                    (Yes! It was real)
on television   A man stepping
down a ladder onto the moon

while Blacks and women
                    (Gays a little later)
began walking their way
to be equal   have power
see recognition flicker in other's eyes

My father and I never talked
about these things
I don't know how he knew
how to bend clothes hangers
hold one in each fist and

walk slowly until they crossed
telling him and everyone
that there was water there
            just below

QUESTIONS

Did you know your grandmother?

Antonia from Moravia   High cheeks
Dark eyes   Grey hair always in bun

Who were you then?

Who I am now but not   (I thought I was
the girl who lived there in that tiny town)

Was she affectionate?

Eyes seemed kind   Lips
full but pressed together
I can not remember her speaking
I have no memory of her voice

And then?

Grandfather never slept
in their bed after her death
He went to sleep on cot in dining room
Hair brush   mirror   hair receiver
pale beige on dresser top

MY LIFE AS AN INTELLECTUAL

(Title from Miriam Sagan poem)

I have to thank my *sockouch!* brothers
Football, baseball, wrestling always
on the television
Car talk, hunting, guns sprinkled
    all over family meals
My dutiful-maid mother cooking
      baking, canning, scrubbing

My turned-up nose rotated
child body in the opposite direction
With back to all these inglorious
activities legs walked me
into the library where
the Queen of Books swept her
hand toward the stacks, and
told me I could "read anything"

And gratitude especially
to my pink rose wallpaper
in the bedroom closet warmed
by the furnace duct
I pulled up close to this
sweet bonfire in the beastly
woods, grinned and fed myself
book after book

NOT AT HOME

"I am not at home in my hometown"

Marge Saiser

I am not at home in my hometown
It's all too muddy again
One way to the grade school, around
to church on Saturday to confess sin

It's all too muddy again
Puddles of March linger and last
To church on Saturday to confess sin
Sunday in pastel short spring coat

Puddles of March linger and last
Clouds pass as if they don't care
Sunday in pastel short spring coats
Promises whispered by high school girls

It's the truth, it's a lie
One way to grade school, around
lonely Main street holding out arms
I am not at home in my hometown

NO COMPARING

is one of the precepts she's
supposed to be following.
Comparing only carries pain
in its critical arms and jaundiced
eye: What the other guy
or gal has got, what coordinated
outfit she's wearing, his color
scheme walls and appropriate
furnishings. You. Yours can never
top the scale.

Measured at doctor's visit she
appears to be at least one–half
inch shorter. Better to shrug,
reach out for what's offered:
frosted sugar cookie, bout of colitis,
afternoon sex, lawn torn up
by mole. Like the crazy Town
Greeter at Laguna, grey hair
flapping in wind, totter forward,
hand extended, yelling, *Welcome!*
Welcome! Come in!

AFTER FATHER'S FUNERAL

It is Monday. He died on
Thursday. Rosary Friday
night. Funeral on Saturday

with fire truck, empty boots
on back, leading the procession
to cemetery, lunch after in
church basement. Now we

are all going away, like birds
changing seasons, back to
our jobs and homes. His car's
been given to the grandson.

Mother stands on the sidewalk,
beside the winter-bare rose
bushes he planted. Instead
of *Goodbye,* she looks at

back door, straightens her
shoulders, states, *I am
going to do this.* Instead of,
I love you, I say, *I know.*

I WANT

I want a pen that doesn't stick on paper
To say, *Oh, that's okay*, to hurt and loss
and really unclench fingers and insides
To like raucous night noises outside
even when they pull me from
a for-once-pleasant dream
To like from-the-heart off-key singing
To like winter as much as spring
To understand dissonance
To not judge, weigh, evaluate everything
on the opposite side of the scale
of what I already know and like
To unveil eyes
Let life's flood sweep locked-up
heart off its stubborn feet
To dance on through
numbered days
warbling exotic songs
with foreign words
spinning in ecstasy

MUST/OUGHT/SHOULD

We must sometimes read the things
    we hate
    Check them out
    once in a while
and brush and floss our teeth
    although I decided not to floss
I was tired of being good

We must make an attempt to listen
when someone is earnestly speaking
Go outside and bring in that
scampering dog brain
Have it heel and sit

And of course eat our carrots
A multivitamin would be good
and everyone knows we must
    drink water

If someone is drowning
    we should leap in
    flail and paddle our way to them

We should begin at the beginning
    get succinctly to the middle
    tie up all the loose ends and
    have a bang-up conclusion

We really ought to
    plan our funerals
    choose a casket
    select our clothes
    pick out hymns, pallbearers
    flowers

We should exercise
    at least three times a week
    (cardio)
    not smoke cigarettes
    not get drunk

We should not argue
    not forget our prayers
    be nice to our brothers and sisters

We should give money to
    disaster victims
    take our old clothes to the
    Salvation Army
We should not waste food
    (There are starving children
    in Africa   in Asia)

We should memorize the names
    of the presidents
    know all the state capitals
and understand how the three branches
    of the government operate

We should be able to remember
    the names of the books we read
    the plots of watched movies
and recognize all the students we've
    had in classes over the years

We should allow no junk food
    to appear in our shopping carts
Leave our name and phone number
if we hit someone's car
We should not leave our apple
    core in the parking lot

We should shine our shoes
Drink our milk
Collect for the Heart Fund
    from our neighbors
We should rake our leaves

We need to recycle
    Get our flu shot
Send Christmas cards, birthday cards
Bake birthday cakes

We should take down our
    Christmas decorations
    before Easter

Have our teeth cleaned
    twice a year
We should volunteer for the good causes
Support the right political candidates

We should dust our houses
Wash our porches
Water our lawns
Not water our lawns
Pick up walnuts in the yard

We should remember our prayers
Learn to recite poems
    from memory
Not complain (there's always
someone worse off than we are)

We should get enlightened
We should do what we want to do

TWO WAYS

"My favorite door opens two ways
receiving and receiving. My heart. . ." *
flaps and lifts, refuses to stay,
Windows are roses, fragrant art

receiving and receiving. My heart
views its life from far off cloud.
Windows are roses, fragrant art.
Gunshots scream more muffled, than loud.

Heart views its life from far off cloud,
is delighted in moonlight and sun.
Gunshots scream more muffled than loud.
Heart wakes, a gazelle, ready to run,

is delighted in moonlight and sun,
finds sand dollars washed on shore.
Wakes a gazelle, ready to run,
Shedding beauty, possessions, becoming poor.

Finds sand dollars washed on shore.
Sends sad times, happy times in the mail,
Shedding beauty, possessions, becoming poor.
Whatever's offered, heart's not for sale,

Sends sad times, happy times in the mail,
flaps and lifts, refuses to stay.
Whatever's offered, heart's not for sale.
My favorite door opens two ways.

*lines from Li-Young Lee

EASY

"Stand still. The trees ahead and bushes beside you
Are not lost. Wherever you are is called Here."*
And breathing becomes familiar and easy
Paying attention or not you will awake

"Are not lost. Wherever you are is called Here."
Amber-colored gown signifies Hope
Paying attention or not you will awake
Eyes radiating secret discovered deep

Amber-colored gown signifies Hope
Silver shoes begin to glow before moonrise
Eyes radiating secret discovered deep
Swaying with branches becoming breeze

Silver shoes begin to glow before moonrise
Souls who were afraid let themselves be seen
Swaying with branches becoming breeze
Doubts retreat   Possibility remains

•   Quote from David Waggoner

LISTENING TO THE TREES

It takes a lifetime of practice
to get it right, colossal effort
to memorize the language, years
of learning vocabulary of pre-storm
frenzy, soft breeze rustle, punctuation
of afternoon stillness in broiling sun.

There are various melodies for
sunrise greetings and somber dirges
for winter light's early demise.
And then comes the sorrowing song
for leaves leaving. Farewells stuck
in tree's throat. Not all

trees are talkers. Some share
their feelings in silence—
hearts withstanding rain, blizzard
and the buzzing onslaught of time.

FRIDAY

"It is the weather of Sundays"
Lawrence Raab

Certainly not August's typical
dreadful humidity and stinky
breath-snatchings days.
   Across the street the Mexican roofers
hammer, bang, slam,
sing-out a counterpoint
to the neighbor's lawnmower hum
and the highway semi,
cattletruck, motorcycle chorus.
Life is time's motion,
a sing-song rattle-bang.
The leaves on the vine dance
along. A robin call
trails across Sky's face
while Sky tries to decide
if she will weep or dry her eyes.
Weekend is standing at the front gate
poised to enter.

TREES NEED NO APOLOGY

Bald and brave in gale and
cold   Not ashamed of
their season   White bark
shining in winter morning light
Translucent green ribbon
leaves unraveling nip at
spring sky like a puppy bite
like *Take me out to the ballgame*

Umbrella of shade slows
Summer's quick dash to
the water   Let her stand
there humming in her bright
hair   No stopping for Fall's
quick costume change
So everyday—trees go

about their business with
unassuming authority   If
you can hear the joke
they will let you
share the laugh

CHILD ON THE ROOF

Is the house sailing down a swollen river
or sitting tranquil, tanning all brown
and loved in summer afternoon?
Is the child playing Tarzan/Superman,

practicing how to be airborne from
this position not worrying about
how to land? Who will find him
if he does not arrive in time for supper?

Will his puppy miss him? What will
happen to his grandchildren standing
next to earth's ladder ready to start
their steep and slow descension?

Is the roof generous enough to
provide a sheltering hand for building
not able to come in out of the rain?

Is the child praying? Believing this
is the way back to his angel time
or only napping in a place his mother
would never look? We should

call the fire department and stand
outside with the rest of the neighbors
as the truck lumbers up, shudders
to a standstill and waits upon

the ambulance hurrying behind trying
to catch its breath before it proceeds
up the ladder to the child waving
from the roof

PRACTICE

You don't have to
be right
even if you are
It's a genetic weakness
like alcoholism and
other addictions

The I-told-you-
so one of the
first phrases
to form and
fall from the
slippery tongue

So what if you
know the answer
So what if
in the long run
your way
is the true way
and you almost
always know the
correct formula
to accomplish tasks

Practice humming
Practice looking
at the color of flowers
Practice patience
like Penelope
unraveling her
tapestry every
evening while she
waits ten years

for Odysseus to return

Become a strong
silent tree with
swaying branches
in life's sweet breeze

COVER UP

My tiny son spouted forth
in a video we were making,
"The purpose of life is
to cover up!" and popped himself
beneath a blanket not to
reappear for the length of
the recording although he could
be heard giggling under there

And yes, *Cover Up* when we
are cold or tired
Cover Up when we wish
to hide or not to see what
is in front of us occurring
Cover Up when we are not
adequately dressed for public
or the weather

Cover Up those objects
we wish to shelter and protect
Cover Up the secret true stories
which no one should share
Cover Up the lies so no one
will know we fabricated,
prevaricated

Cover Up the rose bush
with an upside down red bucket
when the snow pours down
so profoundly blanketing the ground

WINTER FEET

Slabs of marble ice
like my father's
when my mother felt them
not knowing he had died

WHEN

When the bones go
soft
When the eyes blur
fuzzy
When the leaves fall
              murmur
Blankets will cover us
We will sleep
      with our memories
Images crisp as orange
       sky at sunrise
While the clouds and songs
and children and birds
skip   twitter sing
             up high
             sweet sweetly

LANDSCAPE

"WHEN I THINK OF A LANDSCAPE, I AM THINKING OF A TIME"
Adrienne Rich

When we lived in California
five minutes from Disneyland.
All of our visitors wanted to go.
We were not so interested but
liked the fireworks every night
from our front steps—flowery
expressions decorating the sky
hunched over the freeways: Santa
Ana, La Brea, Newport, and Long Beach.

We read erotic books, had sweet
sex in the hallway in front of the mirror,
drove to the beach on Sunday.
Landlubbers, we learned the language
of ocean, waves kissing shore,
celebrated our anniversary on a street
on a cliff above the water when picnicking
on the beach we forgot about tide and
clambered over rocks, barely escaping.

Few friends, we huddled close
in our small space with landlady's
furniture and borrowed television.
Days and nights were simple—
I learned to make a stew and other
dishes—and close. We bought a
waterbed and played. Cocooned
with Santana, Dylan and the Beatles
for the soundtrack, we woke one
morning to headlines of Helter Skelter
not far away.

THE AFTERNOON BEFORE WE MET

was permeated with orange blossom
April   Not hot   Slight breeze
whispering, *something something*
is about to happen so softly
I only remembered later what
it said   We hadn't yet met

I sat at the top of a curved
walkway in front of a college
dormitory   Exams over   The year
almost finished but still
to come, the opening act of
a full-length story

Time was preparing to stop itself,
musicians tuning up and the special
effects technicians figuring out how
to shower all those stunning sparkles
into the scene when the curtain
began to rise

BELL

I went to first grade
at a school up the hill,
not too far from home.

My brothers attended
the Catholic school across
town, too far my parents

said, for me, young for
school and their only girl.
I knew nobody there.

At recess the first day
I sat on the cement steps
instead of running to play.

I knew nobody. The ruddy-
cheeked janitor, Mr. Dooley,
came and sat next to me.

We talked quiet as the kids on
the playground leaped and screamed
and at the end of recess

Mr. Dooley turned and smiled.
How would you like, he asked,
to ring the bell? Holding

out the big brass thing
like a special golden trophy.
And, boy, did I let it chime

and bong, tolling it as if
I were announcing Jesus
coming. The kids (I knew
nobody) stopped and ran to me.

THRILLING

Holy Saturday service
after the covered gloomy statues
                of Holy Week
and only wooden clappers
                at the Consecration
when the host is lifted high
                above the congregation.

On this Eve of Christ's Resurrection
    all the bells awake.
Now when the priest elevates
    the God-round wafer
the communion bells peal,
    clappers cough and clap,
and someone pulls the rope
    on the sleeping bell in the tower.
It's prolonged gong vibrates the night
            —promising—in the morning—
    Easter light.

SIN

"She disliked being told she was a sinner"
Lawrence Raab

They didn't actually call her a sinner
but there was much discussion of sin
Original sin, of course, everyone born with
it because Eve then Adam ate the apple
Some feminists say that myth is about sexuality
and women's being the root of all evil in the
world (Woman, cover your head! In the Middle
East cover everything and stay in the house)

Christ died on the Cross for your sins we
were told in grade school again and again
But still the baby had to be baptized to remove
the stain of sin from her soul   If the child died
without that ritual she would go to Limbo,
denied God's presence for all eternity

My grandmother kept after my parents until we
had our son baptized   *I'm not promising to
raise him Catholic,* I said to the priest   *If you
want to welcome him into the community of
God I'd go for it.*   He agreed.   I picked our Hindu
friend and my mother, the most devout Catholic,
for godparents   *East and West,* I explained

And then there was Mortal Sin and Venial Sin
Mortal Sin could relegate you to Hell for Eternity
I was sure I'd never do anything so serious—Murder?
And what else could possibly be so bad?   I wasn't
sure when I began dating where exactly petting
came on the scale, but I wasn't going to ask

SHE

> "The meaning of life is milk"
>
> Chogyum Trunpa Rimpoche

I like milk but I don't drink
milk so you kids can have it
SHE said *But Mom* I wanted
to say—but we did not talk back
to SHE—*I don't even like milk*
You can have mine But *No*
Milk is good for you
Drink your milk!
White consistent grace
that they could afford
Mostly

We were fed enough
and loved as well as they had learned
from stony parents absorbed in
their own stories of suffering and work

Why did SHE have to scrub floors
on her black bruised knees?
Why did SHE never take a drink?
(*It makes me dizzy*)
The ill-fitting shoes from the rummage sale
Her delight in unearthing *cute*
hand-me-downs for me

No I said and *No* and *No*
I want PINK I said *for*
my new bedroom SHE gave in
Took for her room the color blue

And SHE said she would
get her reward in Heaven
Rich people SHE'D smile
They already got theirs on earth

WEDDING MARCH

He looks as if he's received bad news
walking her up the aisle
her suntan illuminating
her white linen gown
deepening her turquoise eyes

He dark suit
Arrow straight ahead
Nothing here to smile about
               giving away your daughter
               to this short guy
                    Who-knows-who-he-is
Steady
Steady as he goes

She lists a little to the left
Wobbling
Not totally certain
about this new life
she is on her way to

They move like unrelenting time
               on their way to the altar
               to Destiny there waiting
                    anywhichway

INEVITABLE

It was inevitable
    becoming my mother

In Colorado video
    son films me
           row row rowing
           picnic table boat
           with my cane (for now
                  only a sprained ankle)

but it's an act
    my mother would have performed
    and my countenance is melting
    like Dali's watches

Always wanted
    her dark eyes
    black hair
    olive complexion
           but I'm Aryan
           with Grandpa's
                blue eyes

Now though
    her gaunt face
    skinny arms
           (I don't remember hers
              so wrinkled)
rise through me
a pentimento
           She's me underneath

WHY I BECAME A VEGETARIAN:

Because on a trip to California in the 70's
we went into a little temple called *Love
Animals Don't Eat Them* Dogs and cats
were wandering in and out

Because it was the time of Euell Gibbons
Stalking the Wild Asparagus (He died
from cancer and everyone shook their heads)

Because our friend Allen who is sort of
nuts was reading about health food and
vitamins and health and poison and talking
talking talking about it all the time
He came over with his new book on juicing
and he and Bob juiced every fruit and
vegetable in the refrigerator filling gallon
jars with thick brown liquid with blobbing
bits floating in them

Because there was *Diet for a Small Planet*
and we had the realization there wasn't
enough meat to feed the whole world,
because we feed grain to cattle who could
just eat grass and the grain could go to people
There isn't enough land to grow beef
for the whole world but there is enough
land for grains and combining foods to
make complete protein Beans and rice
together are complete protein Spinach
has 27 times the amount of protein as
meat If you add an egg it's complete

Because we read vegetarian cookbooks
like *The Grub Bag* with delicious recipes

like cucumbers in sour cream and essays
like the one advocating if people were made
to eat what they killed there would be less
murder

Because it was the 70's
Because we were flower children
and that's what you did

We made our own granola
We sent for a culture in the mail
and made our own yogurt on
a hot plate added frozen strawberries
This treat was exceeded only by
homemade ice cream churned ourselves
in a crank-handled wooden freezer
with rock salt melting the ice

I bought bread pans and the *Tassajara
Bread book* Studied recipes We bought
a mill to grind our wheat berries to
make flour I baked several loaves of
bread at a time with Bob complaining
that it didn't taste like his mother's,
his grandmother's, rye bread

I made sunflower seed cookies with
oatmeal and raisins

We started a food coop and had
to work there unloading the truck
from Blooming Prairie each month
Pouring oil and syrup into smaller jars,
glomming natural peanut better into small
containers, sacking nuts and dry beans,
slicing huge slabs of cheese into manageable
chunks

Because we believed it was healthy and
cooking this way with spices was more
delicious and interesting that sinewy,
tough meat without much flavor

Because this was the time of communes,
of free love, of pot and LSD, of peace
and love and flowers
and vegetables

This was the time of Primal Scream,
Of Rolfing, of John and Yoko,
Of Jackson Browne, Neil Young, *Hey Jude*

This was the time of massage and touching
Of women's *Consciousness Raising*, Women's
Lib, of men staying home sometimes to
care for the babies

Of hope and vegetables and we
really don't need to eat animals

And *All We Need is Love*
Maybe It's the Time of Man
We were *Searching for a Heart*
of Gold in the eggplant
and in the zucchini

PACKING HER UP

We left her wedding ring and
new diamond my father bought her
not long before. After all, he wanted
her to have them. Also, we pinned
a pendant her granddaughter gave her
with pictures of her great granddaughters
onto her chosen (Fiftieth Anniversary) dress.

We added a decoupage plaque with
a poem I wrote about her, "not knowing
she was pretty." Bob maneuvered
a lily into her cold hand. She had told
him near the end, "Just put a lily in
my hand and close the lid," so he did.
Her name was Lillian.

Finally, my brother tucked a baggie in
beside her of her famous Christmas
cookies he'd been saving in his freezer.
Equipped as fine as any Egyptian
pharaoh she was ready to go, sailing
on her leaden barge into eternity.

"WHAT IS YOUR MOTHER TEACHING YOU?"
Question asked by Suzanne Kehm

My mother without a body
for all these years. She
is so see-through clear.
She is so lit from within.

She is weightless as fall air,
no breeze. House plant
leaf falling on carpet.
Her grandchildren heaved

her through snow so
she could nestle in
beside her mate, no
more bickering.

Her nightly dream train
has left the station.
Departed now to Further-
Away-Without-Commentary.

Red zinnia, feathered pink
cloud.   White bird in
bare tree.

WHEN YOU ENTER. . .

When you enter Istanbul you drive under ancient Roman aqueducts.
This time there's an enormous banner flapping for Guns and Roses.
You will not be able to get tickets. It's worth coming to Turkey for
the flat-domed bread sold from carts everywhere, next to lamb
roasting on the spit. Some sheep stand on verdant hills marked
with a stripe of pink or green down their bony backs. These are
the animals that will be sacrificed for Id.

Do not miss the Cisterns—Roman pillars, underground, half-submerged
in colored water from lights shining in the dark echoey cavern. This is
where the water was stored and now it vibrates with high music. As
sacred here as in the Blue Mosque where you kneel, touch your forehead
to the tiles knowing, *It's all God, all the same God* even though next
stop is Hagia Sophia, which was a mosque, then a Christian church, and
after another conquest a mosque again. Islamic sacred images painted
over by Christian, by Moslem once again, like complicated human
layers which we try to keep shedding to get down to that deep place
where we are all the same.

If you are not too shy there are the baths where you'll discover the body
wonderful, to be pounded, scrubbed, washed, rinsed—human forms of
beauty, all sizes and shapes.

The Grand Bazaar mirrors lifetime on earth, everything you could ever use
for ornamentation—gauzy fabrics, scarves, golden chains, utility of living—
pots and pans, knives, tools all fanned before you, glistening dream of bounty
and barkers calling attention to particular splendid gifts which could be held
in the hand for a while. Spices are mounds of gleaming color and fragrance
at another location.

Istanbul is about the Dervish, those spinners, those weavers, pluckers
of grace, circling sun in center, planets revolving, keeping time with the
pattern of creation—spinning, skirts flared, still here in body manifestation,
emitting joy and light. Open your heart's eye and take it in.

Then proceed upstairs to nourish and fill yourself with green beans, fish, pastries. Turkish coffee, dark and bitter.

Finish at Topaki Palace where some say the remains of Mohammed reside. (In other versions he ascended to Heaven on his steed at the Dome of the Rock). Here a cleric chants heavenly verses unfamiliar, yet you think you heard them before, sweet, haunting, splendid.

EXPECTING

Don't avoid sudden
spring rain   Grab tightly
onto hand of beloved
without words or
hesitation laughing
down front steps
head on   pregnant belly
bouncing into weather
of whatever is to be

MELANCHOLY

Dressed not in black
Maybe navy blue
with a little fringe reminiscent
of the 20's   She wouldn't
dance the Charleston in
public Only at midnight
in front of her mirror Music
turned only moderately loud

She turns in autumn   Not
a brilliant leaf but one
of deepest gold She is
something to have and hold
She will lisp secret murmurings
if you make her feel cherished

Bells ringing softly
The echo of a train whistle
in a town where most of
the young have moved on

Melancholy is referred to
as a woman of *a certain age*
If she is not careful she can
give herself a frozen shoulder
by reaching backward but she
is positively thrilled to be old
enough to have a past even
if others don't find it interesting

It is for her to know
For you to try to find out

Discovery with melancholy always
displays a few lines and wrinkles
around the edges of smooth
ironed linen   Melancholy
likes junk jewelry particularly hanging
blobs of amber-colored things Just
a fine line of frosting across the
top of bar cookies A single sail
on the horizon Slightly stormy

Squawky birds and the flurry
of flapping wings Late at night
from her dreams she wakes up
knowing every time exactly
where she is

Melancholy is a period piece
Holding on to schemes so long
they are out of fashion Not
sadness exactly but a feeling
of knowing this journey in all
its bumps and rubs

Melancholy is a filigree
ironwork fence through
through which to view the passing
afternoon and downtown small
town traffic

Melancholy has a faint odor
of old trunk

SILENCE   WATER   MOON

Bob doesn't like silence   If no one
is talking he feels responsible for filling up
silence as if it were an empty bowl
held out by a saffron-robed monk Please!
Thank You!   And the supplicant will take
what you offer unless of course he is already
full   I remember adults at church dinners
or funeral luncheons turning the white mugs
over as the church ladies approached with
steaming containers of coffee Raymond Carver
after he quit drinking would hold his hand
over his wine glass when waiters approached
Silent Signal for Pass On By without having to say
No Thanks

Do ears get hungry for words when nothing
is being produced by vocal chords? Do
ear channels need to be lubricated
by language to keep them working well?
Should we take the anvil stirrup cochlea
in for a tune-up so they can vibrate at
the proper frequency at social gatherings
be able to plumb the depth and emotion
of classical music like the young woman
who heard Beethoven for the first time
played by her boyfriend on his bedroom
piano and fell in love?

Is silence the other half of sound equally
proportionate in our souls like good and bad
like the devil making up the fourth personage
with God the Father God the Son and the
Holy Spirit or in some versions it's Mary
the mother of Jesus who makes the completed

whole? *Four* stated Carl Jung *Is the number of*
wholeness and individuation becoming a
complete person

 Will we go crazy if there is never any
silence? If we can never enter the beautiful
echoey kingdom within? Why is solitary
confinement considered a severe punishment?
In the 60's experimenters floated in a sensory
deprivation tank with ears stopped no light
no sound body only bobbing with no touch
We used to play that game when we were
kids *If you had to give up one of your senses*
which one would it be I don't remember
anyone choosing to be deaf I had a blind student
who did not use a cane and preferred to walk
around bumping into objects and people He
seemed to be perfectly happy *You talk* he
said *as if color were important but to me*
it moans nothing

I pray for silence in summer's heart when the
motorcycles and crotch rockets explode up
the highway below the bedroom window Waking
me over and over Then I turn to fantasies about
shooting out tires I can live with the cars trucks
semis going about their business but to the crotch
rockets designed specifically to insinuate their
yowl into quiet I would show no mercy River
Highway grows quiet on Christmas Eve Never
even late night in summer are we able to have
a conversation on the porch

A quiet canoe paddled on a summer stream
could be close to silence Brother's speedboat
was designed to roar and rear itself out of the

waves smacking back down hard on the water
rattling your bones   Is something in male genetics
attracted to explosions?   Firecrackers Cherry bombs
Brother blew things up with dynamite Men
rattling from distant rooms Sounds seem to be
about things shattering

When we stayed in a bamboo hut in Bali we
awakened every night to roaring   Took moments
to realize the Indian Ocean below was making
these sounds to break the silence of the night
Temple was mostly silence Hold flower in
folded hands bow open hands to receive
pouring of water Stick blessed piece of rice
to forehead   No sounds or songs of praise
Just silent Moon over ocean   Blue balls
of whizzing light   whirling   *Spirits*
spiritual guide said

Happiest time of childhood was silence in my room
on my closet floor   Sometimes reading mostly
daydreaming *Sitting quietly is also meditating*
said Allen Ginsberg I say to husband *Don't worry*
It's not just your responsibility to fill the gap
I know I know he says *but I get anxious*   .

Friend Natalie and I sat a Seven Day Retreat in
silence   I worried about going to my tent to get
socks because my feet would get cold About
getting an umbrella because it was going to rain
Noticing that guy up there was kind of cute and
finally getting madder and madder because I
had come there to have a God Experience and
all I was doing was getting an aching back and
pinched legs watching my breath

Equal parts day and night in Bali at the Equator
Sun sizzles into sea
Green flash
Silence

"MOST THINGS THAT ARE IMPORTANT LACK A CERTAIN NEATNESS"   Mary Oliver

A man is not a tulip.
Children are no longer taught to write cursive.

I have five friends with birthdays.
Ernest Hemingway was an asshole.

Husband is spraying insecticide on the flowers.
My friends bought a ranch.

I am going to India.
I transplanted the parsley.

There are wild fires in Colorado.
There is flooding in Duluth.

Everything has to do with everything else.
Incense gives me migraines.

Autism appears to be more prevalent.
The shyest person was asked up to the stage.

The 4th of July is the middle of summer.
Gardens and dreams are unconscious messages.

Brilliant! Brilliant!
Cobalt blue and deep red.

He makes beauty out of junk.
To everything there is a season.

AUGUST
PLATTE RIVER CABIN

Canopy of cottonwood tree,
filigree of tinkling arrow leaves
through which to view
the last blue of day sky
going now down Time's river.

JUST OUTSIDE

DIAGONAL CROSSING

Pedestrian stands
meditating on passing cars
until one   like the chosen
thought   halts   A hand
waves for her to go

She goes   on into the day
Time gone on around the corner
and her girlhood patent
leather shoes leave too
Walking the opposite direction

RESCUE

I'm coming   Hold on I yell
racing as fast as my aging body
bad back will allow up
the basement steps to the kitchen
up the hall steps to the bedroom
where you lie in our big bed
(I've departed to the lower
regions because of your deep-night
                    train roar)

The dream still holds you hostage
and you are still sounding your
night time sirens when I, Superhero,
burst through the door to your aid.
I'm here I announce   *It was a*
big pig! you mumble.

WHEN YOU SPEAK

"When you speak I don't listen"

Marge Saiser

I listen most of the time
Almost all the time
but you have *so* much to say
and you are extremely careful
about not leaving out any details
so we will understand what
happened before the story
began and where the world
went and is after the story
is over   Sometimes my ears
sag   It's hard to keep up
Sometimes because you
are so careful having to put
the needle down on the precise
spot to begin the beautiful
sonata you forget what exactly
the story was you meant to tell
and sometimes by then I forget
to listen

UNSUSPECTING

While you are reading and I
daydreaming the passing years
are tucking our lives into
their strange vanishing closets,

performing Houdini magic
on our brains and switching
out our familiar hands with
those of our old parents. Pity!

OCTOBER 1945

The war is over
And Johnny comes marching home
And a sailor bends a woman backward
in a kiss which goes on forever
Confetti falls from Heaven
Soldiers troop into VFWs
across America trying to wash
away horror scenes, guns and wounds
with sloshing beer and tight lips
The medicine doesn't work so well

Rosy the Riveter closes the door
on the munitions plant opens her
kitchen door oven door back to
her position cookies and ironing

A new generation comes Boom
Booming out of the hospital
cascading waves across the landscape
Those who'll learn
Not to trust anybody over thirty
To make love not war
To give peace a chance

These hot rod kids who grew
up under the mushroom cloud
Who practiced hiding under
their school room desks
Whose neighbors built shelters
under the ground   stocking them
with canned goods and water
Who had to at first be careful
in swimming pools in summer
but whipped that Old Cripple Polio

and grew up to hitchhike like
Kerouac and Cassidy on their
own roads across America

Who tripped other ways too
into surreal dream and scenes
dripping with colorful skirts
and fringed vests beads and
head bands   Jimi Hendrix
Wa Wa screeching Allegiance
to America

America we questioned,
What are you doing killing
people in their own civil war?
We disagreed about the dominoes
falling We wanted to talk about
love and sex And aren't we all
brothers and sisters?   And isn't
love free?   And shouldn't we
taste it all with everybody?

Hats and gloves came off
in churches   Folks decided
to sit in the sunlight or go
surfing instead of sit in pews
And women went out of the
kitchen again   to law school
med school to become bosses
in companies

My mother still canning green
beans and trying not to have
people notice her
God came back to life
Charlie Starkweather and Carol

Ann Fugate committed their slaughter
before Charlie's Manson's insane
orgy of killing

America puffed up big with money

Blacks sat on the bus Stood up
to oppression And marched
with interlocked arms

It was all *Blowing in the Wind*
Great ones blown away too soon
out of their stories
While I tried in my pink bedroom
to worm my way into this big
movie through books stacked
up from the library   not knowing
there was someone
glistening and funny
on his way
to walk with me

PORCH TALKS

I'm not that word, he says.
I've just said he's loquacious
during our porch talks—
turning our chairs to face
each other, having discussions
as we sip beer and semis roar by
on the highway.

Usually these talks get around
to sex and what's happened
to us over these forty-eight years
of down and ups.

I still think he's pretty talkative
sometimes, especially in an altered state.
He disagrees, is slightly miffed,
like both of us, about most issues,
while we love love each other
on down through the tree rings
of time.

CAN'T REMEMBER

She can't remember what season they are in
This is what comes of traveling in Winter

Almost spring but there is much confusion
Fever Few and lilies starting to stand

Too soon Too soon she warns and wonders
if fall-like days in South were just a dream

Moon in sky in afternoon round pie
Pocky face winking at Sun still high

What's to become of all this love?
Misplaced goals to want to know

What is God?
Where is She?

What are we to do about unlearning
alphabets of fear and hate?

O SPARROWS

Whither are you going this new day?
Menage-a-trois first on wire outside window
Now conferring in twiney trumpet vine

Are you discussing moon turned red
then disappearing from autumn night
It came back later   Maybe
it woke you with its wealthy light

Ignoring semi traffic on highway
Never taking a turn on green porch swing
I know you know something I wish
to discover but miniature wings brush away

the question and you pilot steady
toward cloud island in pale lake sky

WE NAP WITH THE DEAD

In our hometown cemetery,
Memorial Day, we've made
our annual pilgrimage fulfilling
the vow to my mother. "No one
will come to visit *me* when
I'm dead," she puffed as we
trooped among the departed,
prim and quiet in their rows.
I promised, "I will," but added,
"You aren't going to be there,
you know, in the ground."
She nodded.

Now, suddenly exhausted after
marching through regiments of
great grandparents, grandparents,
uncles and aunts, and our immediate
genitors, we collapse into our car.
"Lay back," I urge to my beloved,
lowering my seat. "Let's just rest."

On our backs, gazing at cerulean sky
empty except for one tiny cloud,
a couple floats by with a bouquet.
"Ah," I murmur, knowing now how
the dead feel as warm bodies pass
on errands of duty, love, and remembrance
among and above them

ALL DAY INERTIA

All day inertia holds her
        like gravity holds us
        to the planet's heart so
        we do not fly into blankness

Not yet   Not yet

        Systems failing in the
                ship of body
        but not so many or so profoundly
        we cannot continue on course
        The course to finally dock
                into Harbor

                        Home Home at last

but for now
        only pausing momentarily
        still reading this same book
        even tho' it's not interesting

too much bother
to rev up the engines
        to move on to
        some other little port
                for a while

NEVER THOUGHT

She never thought about sleep
She was good at it
In college dorm mates gathered
around her single bed
speculating whether or not
                    she was dead
(so still   never moving)

Now sleep comes
                but mostly goes
Awake after a couple hours
        she does the review
    No caffeine late in the day
    Toilet before bed
    Does her hip hurt?
            Did the pain wake her?

Oh! If she can just hang on
            to the dream train
        picking up speed as it
            rounds the bend—
just a shard will do—
        to allow her to jump back
        aboard   Let the story continue

But sometimes
      Dream's scary
         Even frightening
If only unpleasant she'll
        grab for the caboose

Waiting to be unconscious
      Awake even after herbs—
      once in a while benadryl—

she practices:
        Eyes Tight
        DO NOT check the clock!
Do not allow mind machine
        to begin it's revving
                remembering
   Recall
           Reverb   *Is that the birds??*

WRITING A SONG

I am writing a song for
the robin hopping on snow pile
Where'd the grass go?
Deep red spears of peony
pushing up up even under
dislodged rock

I am writing a song for
we chose these bodies
put them on
smiled at the movie
where we watched them grow
peeking into what was to be
peering into ponds from
up high Narcissus-like
loving our reflections

I am writing a song for
legs that still move though
hips are achey   neck pain
the spring that isn't
how we thought it'd be
things collapsed and
caved in back there
in the yard where we
thought they were stationary
Goddess statue lost her head

I am writing a song for
hold on to your hat, your
noggin, your mind   Singing
is a formula for wending
your way through life's
puzzling maze   Tra-la

FINISHING THE BOOK

Technically there's some blank pages
because traditionally I write on the right;
leave the left blank to take notes, make
lists, rewrite a stanza. Then sometimes
too when my notebook is full I can still
find a page or two to write something
without tearing the cellophane off a new
blank black leather notebook with unlined
white pages or, more bother yet, driving to
Hobby Lobby to buy a new one. I buy them
one at a time—this is my tradition. It would
be easier to at least get two at a time but I've
always done the ritual of one at a time from
the Hobby Lobby aisle which I can never find
back in the art section with canvases, easels,
paints and pencils. Sometimes they are on sale,
especially then, I think I should get at least two,
but I stand my ground, don't back down, knowing
this is what's been working all these years—one
new notebook at a time. I'd rather not get them
at Hobby Lobby because of their political stand on
Obama Care or birth control provisions in the
insurance plans. I used to know but have forgotten
and I don't know where else to get an unlined leather
writing notebook in my small town so I continue to
buy it there anyway just like I drink Coors beer
anyway even though there was some politics (John
Bircher?) but we couldn't get Coors in Nebraska
for a long time. Schlitz or Pabst kept them out so we
were jubilant when we finally could. I like the taste
so much better than Bud although occasionally I feel
guilty about drinking it, enjoying it—like enjoying the
warmer weather in winter when it's probably from
Global Warming. There was some issue too about

Tommy Hilfinger or that other clothes brand I like
sexualizing young people in their ads but I can't
remember which one for sure any more.
I got the leather notebooks to preserve the writing
to have it all together so I could always find the
piece of writing I was looking for. My husband's
idea really—He built me shelves for storing them
in the basement, is proud of them, gives tours to
show them off. I was showing some writing students. "Don't
you ever tear out a page?" one asked. "Why would I want
to do that?" I answered. She looked aghast. But, now with
a granddaughter arriving, old age approaching and after
that the Inevitable, I'm thinking to make a fire to throw them in.
Why would I wish to leave these mewlings, ramblings, rantings,
whinings, sexual secrets behind me. No, I think it would be
fine to make a fire, to *Burn Them, Baby*. Burn them gone.

SHE MEANT   (MOSTLY ASLEEP AT 11 PM)

She meant to buy a pickup truck
Get some shit-kicking cowboy boots
Go at least one time to the circus
Learn how to sail without banging
  into other boats in the dock
Wind sail

Surf the Indian Ocean
Jump out of an airplane
Fly a helicopter
Be the richest man in the world
    Drink Corona beer
Be thirsty
Marry the richest man

Get a plan
Get a life
Get out of bed in the morning
Forget that she didn't have
   a date for prom
Suck stuffed dates
Go on a date to dinner and a movie
Have him pay for it

Buy designer clothes
Grow fingernails
Get sick Get well Toss around
   the ink well
Begin again
Begin over and over
Never ever be through beginning

Oh where oh where has my little dog gone
with his ears cut short and his tail . . .

Find the three blind mice and
see how they run
Help the Farmer out of the Dell

Eat more popcorn
Put sugar on everything
Find someone to wash windows
Know every day which way
the wind blows
So long   Farewell   Goodbye

It is only a rehearsal
for her life in the alternate universe
where she means to live
Has meant to live there

Buy a house
Pack her bags
    Buy scotch tape
Let Jesus down from the Cross

Forget about you
You long lazy blues guy

Sleep when you sleep
She dreams most of the night
That beautiful death-imitating
deep slumber of no dream   No deal

She always meant to look up
the existence of God   She meant
to by now know everything
not to have to worry anymore

about not catching a taxi
or finding her way around town

stopping for the train
rumbling down the narrow highway
stumbling out of bed

Oh Lord, don't buy me anything
I want it for free
    just between you and me

Catch the midnight toad
Stay still when the furry creatures
hurry by another way   We doubt
we will ever look back   Therefore
this is the end   She always meant
to write in her sleep

MOON FROWNS

The stars just won't straighten themselves
Where are we supposed to be?
asks the one in front of the pack
and what is all that howling
down below?   When smoke clears
they can make out crumbled cities,
bodies, a few souls running
in the semidark

AGAIN

The sky is once again December
grey. It forgot in the endless
autumn it was an old lady.

Sunbright hair washed to its
suddenly-remembered age.
Clouds overhead clucking,
You thought you could escape?

Sure, there are times of reprieve
when Inevitable seems to be
of no more importance; but
the World clears its throat,

stands up straight and goes
on its way handing out packages
of harshness, bundles of *too late*.

I DO NOT THINK MY DEAD WILL RETURN

My Dead have not yet gone

Mother came every night
Hovering   Face close to mine
Up Close   Until I did a ceremony
Ate some of her Christmas cookies
Took her sweetness   Then she was
a step removed in dream   Covering
the bed in golden silk   Putting
Resurrection lilies by my head

Dad came regular but would not
speak when asked how it was there
where he was living   He left again
in an alien ship of light

Friend Pat shortly after death
got on the bus tottered to
the back where I was sitting
Said *I know you think I'm
Dead; it's not like that*

Grandma came many times
When I said she was dead
and scaring me she said
Don't be silly

Yoga friend said *Hop like this!*
and turned into a toad—his home
the Sacred Toad Ashram

Gary graduate of Navy Academy
said *I haven't much time* but showed
me a room wallpapered with the seal of US Navy

Cindy has not come to me
She said nothing in her life
had prepared her for this dying
Wanted to learn to meditate but
brain tumor so strong-willed we
could only read poetry She left on
How to Paint Sunlight by Ferlinghetti

After the bat loose and flapping
I was afraid in the dark Not
of dying but what might come
before

When Ramana Maharshi's students
begging him dying not to leave them
He said *Where would I go?*

Aunt Addie died last week.
She said *It's so hard to cross over*
but the water is so beautiful
Daughter Patty said *Get in!*
She said *I'm trying* after telling
us she remembered the tomatoes
at our wedding reception fifty years
ago Could see them on her plate

My guide says *When you're alive*
you are in the body looking out
When you die you are on the
outside looking in

All my dead peep through my
window eyes I invite Mother
to see great granddaughter who
says *Outside Outside* all the time

yells for milk but then says *Please*
Yells *Doggie Doggie* to the seven
foot elk but when they come
closer *Buddy Buddy*

THE END

"Dance me to the end of love"
                    Leonard Cohen

Oh! She would like one more
cup of coffee—always a limit
because of migraines—and last
champagne bubbles on her tongue—

that taste denied so long—
and Yes! finally some chocolate
deep and dark and why not
have all surviving lovers come

for a final tryst—all lined up
separate or all one big bang
humpty-hump just for the
hell of it (because Heaven no

doubt will be more staid)   Rock
music blasting, poets yelling
rhythmic phrases and rich images,
cardinal tweet, semi honk
and a long last moan of
                    train whistle

DYING

Nothing
to be done
except
scoop up
handful
of withered roses
and sail
on pink
scent
into Eternity

IN LADEKH, INDIA

Butter lamps glint and flit
like lined-up fireflies
in this dim monastery. "I've
been here before," I say.
Friend says, "It's like church."

But eons and incidents swirl
just past my seeing, remembering
themselves. A song called Home
floats from within. "No," I say,

Lifetimes before," and it's where
I will come again when Soul
is free to chart its own
love course. Here.

This dark heart.
Raw red flame.

JUST OUTSIDE

Joy has come to live
    in their house

oh heart heart heart
oh bleeding drops of red

Joy is standing on the red porch
    under the golden roof
next to Grandpa's green porch swing

Softly singing
Then more loud
    All this time they thought
    it was the cars and trucks
    sighing and whizzing
    along the highway river
but it was Joy humming
drawing close
pressing its nose up against
the window
    Waiting

They didn't know it was Joy
    just outside the door
They thought it was
    the dogs barking
    lawnmower chirping happily
    as it chomped down
    its weekly large meal of grass

They didn't know Joy
didn't know how to read
    or write
They thought maybe it was

a secret passage in another language
inside a book hidden on
an upstairs shelf

They didn't know Joy was an
          easy recipe in an open cookbook
          on the wooden kitchen table
She didn't need a new stove after all
It wasn't necessary to preheat the oven
No assembly needed

All they had to do was tug
          at the bow
pull the colored paper off
There stood Joy all shining
          like the Christmas child

I belong to you Joy said
I am yours
All you have to do
          is open your arms
          Reach out
          Relax

Let us tell each other a story
about how Happiness has come
to town hitched a ride with Joy
Joy is so to speak her boy

Oh let them in
Let them begin
          It's been a long time coming
          It will be a long time gone

www.ingramcontent.com/pod-product-compliance
Lightning Source LLC
Chambersburg PA
CBHW020211090426
42734CB00008B/1017